A Special Gun for Elephant Hunting

Poems

by

Howie Good

Printed in the United States of America

First Printing 2012

ISBN 978-0-9855291-1-6

Dog On A Chain Press
c/o Beasley Barrenton
503 Silverleaf Rd.
Zionville,NC 28698

For ordering information or all other inquiry
dogonachainpress@yahoo.com
http://www.lulu.com/spotlight/beasleybarrenton

for contributor credits/permission see back page(s)

It seemed the kind of life we wanted. Charles Simic

"I thought about something from O'Hara...then I looked for something from Berrigan...but whoever it may be that decides to read these poems, they can just start where the poems are, that'll suffice."
A letter from the Editor's desk-

RIMBAUD IN AFRICA

The route you traveled
is no longer in use.
There is just this light,

scattering.

LIVING AN ANIMAL LIFE

musk or ostrich plume
or ivory
I paced and muttered through curiously longer nights
why force a giraffe into a flower pot,

I keep thinking

the gods respond to questions like these in the summer
when all the windows are open.

THE WORST

It's true,
I always imagine
the worst,
the small circus
in my head
closing,
the bearded lady
forced to shave
twice a day,
the lion dying
of hunger
under the swing set
in a neighbor's
backyard,
people saying
about me
that he used
to write poetry.

FOG AREA

I'm dressed in a French-cut suit
the color of a cloudy day.

A cadaver dog approaches,
hesitant and mannerly.

There's no effective pill.
There never was.

WHAT LOVE IS THIS

and when I fill you, you're Atlanta
smoldering in ruins, and I'm a cart
loaded with the groaning wounded.

your breath taste far away from everywhere.

We're twelve grains of gunpowder
floating mightily through the air.
We make rocks leap and split.

our new kind of pearl handled combustion.

the circus bears must dance their spooky minuet.

THE WILDERNESS

1
In the sudden start, somebody lost his hat. Nobody stops to pick it up. Home is always further on.

2
Business is down. The news is bad. There's a haze between me and the rest of the world. Only one thing left to do, the fat lady says – sing.

3
My only choice of companions is savages or imbeciles. Tonight we'll water our horses in the Tennessee River. The stars will be hard to see, every bush hung with shreds of bloodstained clothing.

BLASPHEMIES OF A BARKING DOG

So much has disappeared. This is a land without mysteries and escape, left in silence.

Here is a gaunt man in drab clothing, wearing an overcoat and walking a frantic little dog.

The dog is barking blasphemy, the man has the small, hooded eyes of Joan of Arc's inquisitor. She is sitting in the corner by herself, hands over her face.

THE FOUR SEASONS

1 Autumn

A matter not of character,
but chemicals,
I tell anybody who asks,
pointing at the sun
as if any minute
it weren't going to be night.

2 Winter

The road just ends.
I can't go back,
you can't go forward,
and we can't stand still.

3 Spring

Sun breaking through. . .
The shrunken old woman

who just about fills
a child's rocking chair

threads the beads of rain
left in her lap to make

one last silver necklace.

4 Summer

And when a girl opens
her mouth to speak,
the booming of her heart
escapes into the air.

STRANGE WEATHER

1

You used to like your job painting the eyes on dolls. You wake before the alarm, the wind talking gibberish.

2

The sun, big feet, big hands, dirt under the nails, is selling key rings and other trinkets in the street. But why go on? Whatever the time of year, dead leaves always seem to be falling.

3

It's too hot for curiosity. The heat tortures us night and day. Broken and crumbly, what may be a corpse floats over warehouses and docks and empty, upturned faces. This isn't the pain I experienced at birth.

4

In front of me wrapped in clouds you step naked and small from the claw foot tub. Ancient voices of children sing outlawed songs. With what may be a smile, a terrible rain begins.

THE LAST BEAUTIFUL EVENING

I like how your legs
wrap around me
a lapse of the last beautiful evening,

how I'm the day world
delving into shadow,

how,

when we toss
as would a small green boat
on a vast yellow sea,

everything is bathed
in violet.

MICE IN A FISH TANK

Someone has posted a picture of Somali child soldiers on telephone poles around town.

The only store open is out of the pills you take.
You can't fall asleep without dreaming you're calmly being stabbed.

When you leave home the next morning, the mice you keep in a fish tank dash their heads against the glass.

Your office-mate sulks over your imagined slights. *What do you think I should be for Halloween?* he later asks.

DECEMBER, LEWIS BAY

I take a walk
down the beach,

gray and empty,
the way I like it,

only a few gulls,
clowns and magicians

and pretty maids
with an alarmingly

haunted look
in their eyes,

what's that say
about me?

THROUGH A GLASS BRIGHTLY

The best music is inaudible,
a little boy pedaling his bicycle
after a delivery van.

POST-IMPRESSIONIST

A farmer hid you from the Germans.
You spent long, empty hours curled up inside a flower,
resigned to headaches and insomnia.

When you returned to Paris after the war,
the people on the street were just shadows.
You had finally discovered the color of the atmosphere.

It was dull yellow, almost pumpkin.

AVIARIES
for Joseph Cornell

1

Waiting for it to burst into bloom, you stare at a tree, rain flying so close that its feathers brush against you.

2

You make a box of the night sky, with constellations of nails; another that resembles the door to a river; and others more like windows, or caskets, or a ballerina who suffers from migraines and talks to pigeons.

3

You were hailing a taxi on the corner of Fifth Avenue and 53rd when you heard the word "beautiful", long, thin, misunderstood. What more could you want? Well, to be guarded on either side by a stone lion.

4

You open the cage of a stuffed green parrot. It takes some people a lifetime to realize that what should occupy empty space is emptiness.

WHO KNOWS WHAT HAPPENS NOW

Gulls have a third eyelid.
I lost my sunglasses.
Blue-eyed people
are supposed
to wear sunglasses.
I shield my eyes
with one hand
and point darkly
with the other.
Gulls crouch like doubts
among the rocks,
the psst of waves
withdrawing.

THE RELIC MUSEUM

A map on the wall suggests our possible whereabouts.
I feel the need to repent,
though not quite sure for what.

In a corner a nickelodeon presents a slow-moving series
of ticking images. It might be of the first time that ballet
dancers rose on their toes.

THE KISS

Your tongue, a rising storm,
finds me. I wish I were a tree
so my branches could shake.

WAITING ON INSPIRATION

I used to imagine you
as the sound of falling water,
then I woke up one morning
with someone else's
heart breaking in my chest.
I couldn't bear to look
when the colonel cried, "Bayonets!"
and men without an eye
or nose or arm or leg charged.
I knelt down and drank
from the dog's bowl
just to have something
to write about.

PERSONAL MYTHS

1

I was born at six in the evening. Rumors that the doctor wore black gloves are untrue. The rivers and lakes were full. My mother put stones in her pocket to keep from floating back up. It was November, and the click of a revolver could stop a heart.

2

I came to a fence and climbed over it and then realized I had forgotten my bag on the other side. There was nothing in the bag I actually needed. I was traveling to a faraway country, where the word for rain was more real than the rain itself.

3

A fluttery bird spoke up. It's what happens sometimes. The sky brightened, but only for an instant.

4

We were friends before we were a couple, but unreliable narrators before we were either. When I opened the door, I found a small Midwestern city, suicidal and dimly lit. I couldn't explain it, not even with complex equations. We agreed to act as if these were things that mattered.

5

Mother dying, the wind said, *come home.* I closed my eyes to rest them. When I looked again, gilt trimmings glittered on military uniforms in the gaslight of the Hotel Brunswick's crowded ballroom. Such people usually leave misleading clues as to their whereabouts. I kept on toward another birthday. Why the shawled whores in the doorways had limbs that had metamorphosed into wings.

6

The road just ends. I enter a house with covered mirrors, buttercups brightening the curtains. Sometimes

I wait to be rescued. Other times I remove the rope myself from around my neck

7
One had a dangerously fast heartbeat. The police knocked one down. One was mathematically eliminated – what you get, I suppose, for asking who wrote Shakespeare's plays. One tilted like a helicopter at takeoff. My dead. There have been years I haven't been able to visit you. There are days like this when that's all I do.

8
You yell from another part of the house that your watch has stopped. Nothing works as well anymore as the perfume of decay. Later a man returning from sleep will wave his arms to ward off marauding dogs. It's night again, I yell back, and the chance of sunshine zero.

FIRE and SWORD

1
Everything you do
with a horse,
Buck says in the movie,
is a dance.

Think of horses,
with blood streaming
from their nostrils,

lying on the ground
hitched to artillery guns,

the sad wind blowing
on a city afternoon.

2
Night closes in.
The bridge sways.

Armies are moving,
using a cane.

3
Dying men, dead men,
some without an arm or leg,
some without heads,
cry themselves to sleep.

MY LIFE and HARD TIMES

1

He comes toward me,
jingling a paper cup.

The kind of books I write
aren't the kind that sell.

2

I stand knee-deep
in the noise of spiders.
Old cuts begin to bleed.

If they won't love me,
an angel is thinking,
they can still fear me.

3

An ungovernable city of chill and gloom.
Every street ends in an ellipsis. . .

Only a stranger, or madman, would stop here.
I step down off the bus.

NOSTALGIA FOR THE LIGHT

The beach is empty, but informers and false witnesses are everywhere.

a silver light filtering through the clouds is flecked with shadows, like the one-eyed cat's good eye or a roadside bomb hidden among the garbage and the weeds obsessively rehearsing what it's going to say.

When it rains, how quickly my pockets fill up with water! I always think the same thing: *You bastards, there are innocent people down here.*

THE KILLING
for Christopher Marlowe

The sight of rain pecking in the gutter was strangely disquieting. Spies were everywhere. Plague, too. You would always regret what happened to the dancing monkeys. Shadows crowded around, so many that you didn't notice the man with freckles on one hand raise the dagger with the other. The blade entered just above your right eye. It's less a story than a situation. You heard many languages being spoken at once, you saw pink flamingos in velvet and gold swirling like clouds against the ceiling.

I HEART ANOMALIES

I fell asleep in the circle of her arms
and woke up years later in exile.
The physics of how are still unclear.

A blue jay
with black feet
flew in
our window.

Things
were neither
better
nor worse.

She asks
if I remember.
I say I do.
I don't.

I hear what sounds
like the pounding of wings.

The next morning,
I find her earring in bed
and poems everywhere.

ANTIDEPRESSANT

To get red,
you need dust
and haze.

Pollution makes
the sunset
so beautiful.

A shadow was combing
its hair in the mirror.
I woke up the next day
with glass in my bed.

An empty car stalled at a light.
Row, row, row your boat.
It was still dark though I did.

I stand at the window looking out.
movement is largely about being still.

From now on,
everything will have
a double meaning,
slightly bullet shaped
and daffodil yellow.

STORY WITHOUT A NAME

1
A big oak tree
blocks the door.
The cunt. And, still,

the mailman
brings the mail.

2
Wednesday is a mystical day.
It leaves everything in,
even the mistakes.
Birds, light, snow, rain,

everything.

ECHO'S BONES
for Samuel Beckett

1
God's stale breath swayed the treetops, the suggestion of a dance. *No,* you replied, *I don't want to.*

2
You weren't cold. You just shivered sometimes.

3
Sunshine, you said, looking up from a whiskey, *is an overrated virtue.*

4
Strangers often commented on your eyes – gull's eyes, someone called them. If you heard, you gave no sign. The sea crashed just outside your door.

5
From the window, you could see the cemetery where your father was "at rest." You weren't interested in stories of success, only failure.

6
There's no such thing as love, you insisted in a loud, drunken voice. *There's only fucking.* Too drunk to negotiate the revolving door, you whirled round and round.

7
An editor asked to see your newest poems. You swam so far out that the others were frightened.

8
The moon rose. So much so, you practiced Chopin on the piano, the notes like men in bowler hats with large heads and no bodies.

9
Grass was trying to grow among the stones. You watched for a while and then shrugged.

10
The sleeping pills that knocked you out at night also kept you in a daze during the day. Jesus wiped the dribble from your chin.

11
The perfect play was one in which there were no actors or director, only the text itself and the despair with which you wanted the audience to leave the theater.

12
A couple of tramps had filched your old, well-thumbed thesaurus. One sentence after another stuttered to a stop. The horizon resembled the chewed stub of a pencil.

13
Everyone had a theory about what you meant by what you said. "Critic" was one of your favorite curses.

14
The laughter of theatergoers verged on rudeness. *Nothing is funnier than unhappiness,* you said.

THE END

The air makes one crazy,
backward fruit, children, seasons,
so violent and so pointless,
a special gun for elephant hunting,
until it's all just a hum,
without winters or summers,
living alone and writing nothing down.

MUTE ARIA

I got just enough
body to keep
a soul in,

and the sun
coming up

the front steps
with a big,
sinister smile,

and cardinals
in the snowy trees.

TWILIGHT

A man in gray
rides a gray horse
toward shore,

broken lanterns
everywhere,

the light bleeding out,
dim and indefinite,

spirits
calling softly to us,
as of old.

My horse trembles.

ANSWERED PRAYER

The drapes have been drawn
against the daylight.
Someone knocks again,
urgently this time.
It could be strangers in masks
or baby-faced angels
or just someone come to tell me
if the world is where I left it
the night before.

Howie Good is a journalism professor at SUNY New Paltz, author of five poetry collections, most recently *Dreaming in Red* from Right Hand Pointing and *Cryptic Endearments* from Knives Forks & Spoons Press. He has a number of forthcoming chapbooks as well, this is his first endeavor with **Dog On A Chain Press.** He has recently returned from Belgium, wits intact, or so he says.

Above photo: Photographer **Gabriel Santerno**, a Dog On A Chain Press mainstay and confidant. Seek her work at gsanterno.com

Inset photo: Photographer *Corrado Dalco* was born in Parma town of Italy. In 1992 *Corrado* moved to Berlin, Barcelona and London, finding immediate success as a fashion photographer for magazines and advertising campaigns. Dog On A Chain Press is grateful that someone as prolific and grand as *Corrado* would even consider a hand out for us, and we are enthralled. www.corradodalco.co.uk

Cover piece**: Christopher Lucania** was born and raised in New Jersey. He is a self-taught artist who works primarily with mixed media on canvas. He focuses on the emotional contrast of victory, redemption, and hope despite tragedy, judgment, and ultimate annihilation. He draws his inspiration from the renaissance, baroque, decaying surfaces, mythology, and historical prose, somehow radiating both beauty and despair. Christopher can be contacted via www.christopherlucania.com

ACKNOWLEDGMENTS

The author wishes to thank the editors of the following publications in which poems in this book originally appeared, sometimes in different form: *A-Minor, Pure Slush, trans lit mag, RiverLit, pressboardpress, Rain Dogs, Bigger Stones, Bending into Light III, Scud Magazine, Safety Pin Review, Other Room Journal, Marco Polo, Poydras Review, Rumble Magazine, Stone Highway, Right Hand Pointing, Awosting Alchemy, Salt., Exclusive_Magazine, MICROW, Bartleby Snopes, Mad Rush, A Small Good Magazine, elimae, Waterhouse Review, Red Lightbulbs, Rufous Salon, Martian Lit, and Boiler Journal.*

Dog On A Chain Press would like, as always, to raise a glass and extend a gallant praise to all of those who have hunkered down and helped us feed the hyena. We will have to make the bunker bigger (if not add a few foxholes along the way) and we are indeed willing to do just that. We once again invite you into "the subtle apocalypse we all dream of". Pura Vida-

www.ingramcontent.com/pod-product-compliance
Lightning Source LLC
Chambersburg PA
CBHW030311030426
42337CB00012B/667